Looking Up!

Torrey Maloof

Consultants

Sally Creel, Ed.D.
Curriculum Consultant

Leann Iacuone, M.A.T., NBCT, ATC
Riverside Unified School District

Jill Tobin
California Teacher of the Year
Semi-Finalist
Burbank Unified School District

Image Credits: p.9 Andrew Woodley/agefotostock;
p.8 (top) Yellow Dog Productions/Getty Images;
pp.5, 14 iStock; pp.13 (top), 18–19 (bottom) NASA;
pp.20–21 (illustrations) Chris Sabatino; all other
images from Shutterstock.

Library of Congress Cataloging-in-Publication Data

Maloof, Torrey, author.
  Looking up! / Torrey Maloof; consultants, Sally Creel,
Ed.D. curriculum consultant, Leann Iacuone, M.A.T., NBCT,
ATC Riverside Unified School District, Jill Tobin, California
Teacher of the Year Semi-Finalist, Burbank Unified School
District.
    pages cm
  Audience: K to grade 3.
  Includes index.
  ISBN 978-1-4807-4572-8 (pbk.)
  ISBN 978-1-4807-5062-3 (ebook)
  1. Astronomy—Juvenile literature. I. Title.
  QB46.M258 2015
  522—dc23
                                              2014013187

Teacher Created Materials
5301 Oceanus Drive
Huntington Beach, CA 92649-1030
http://www.tcmpub.com
ISBN 978-1-4807-4572-8

Table of Contents

Look Closely

When you look up at the night sky, what do you see? Do you notice the twinkling stars? Can you spot the shining moon? It is important to look closely.

Observe

To **observe** (uhb-ZURV) means to watch closely. What do you observe in the night sky?

When you look closely, you learn more.
Your five **senses** can help you learn. Use
your eyes to watch closely. Use your ears
to listen carefully.

touch

taste

Five Senses

You have five senses:
touch, taste, sight,
sound, and smell.

sight

sound

smell

7

Use your hands to feel. Use your nose to smell. You can even use your tongue to taste.

These kids use their senses to observe.

Warning!

Do not smell, touch, or taste anything that can hurt you. Ask an adult first!

Study the same thing in the sky again and again. Look at it from different spots. Watch it at different times. You will learn more this way. You will notice new things each time.

The stars and moon look different each night.

Use Tools

There are tools that can help us observe the sky. A **telescope** (TEL-uh-skohp) is one tool. It helps us see things that are far away. It can even see into space!

This kid uses a telescope.

Flying Telescope

The Hubble telescope flies through space. It sends pictures back to Earth.

A **microscope** (MAHY-kruh-skohp) is a tool, too. It helps us see things that are too small to see with just our eyes. It makes small things look big and clear.

This boy uses a microscope to see small things.

Let It Snow!

Each snowflake is different. We know this because we have looked at them with microscopes.

Make Observations

To observe is to learn. It is important to write what you learn. Take notes. Use **descriptive** (dih-SKRIP-tiv) words. Draw or take pictures. These are called **observations** (ob-zur-VEY-shuhnz).

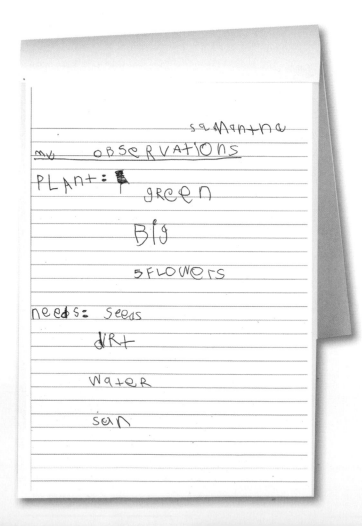

This girl writes her observations.

17

Scientists look closely at things in the night sky. They make observations. They have taught us many things. What will you teach us? What will you observe?

This boy observes the sky with a telescope.

This scientist studies stars through a very large telescope.

Let's Do Science!

How does the moon move across the sky? Try this and see!

What to Get

○ paper and pencil

What to Do

1 Go outside on a day when the moon can be seen.

2 Observe where it is in the sky. Draw a picture of what you see.

3 Wait an hour and go back outside. Observe where the moon is in the sky and draw it again. Do this a few more times.

4 Look at your pictures. What do you notice? Why do you think this has happened?

Glossary

descriptive—using words to tell about things or people

microscope—a tool used to see very small objects

observations—statements about things that you have noticed

observe—to watch and listen carefully

senses—how you get information about the world around you

study—the process of learning about something

telescope—a tool used to see things that are far away

Index

Your Turn!

Observe It

Look up at the night sky and find a star. Observe it. Is its light steady? Does it seem to move? Is it the same size as other stars? Write what you observe in a notebook.